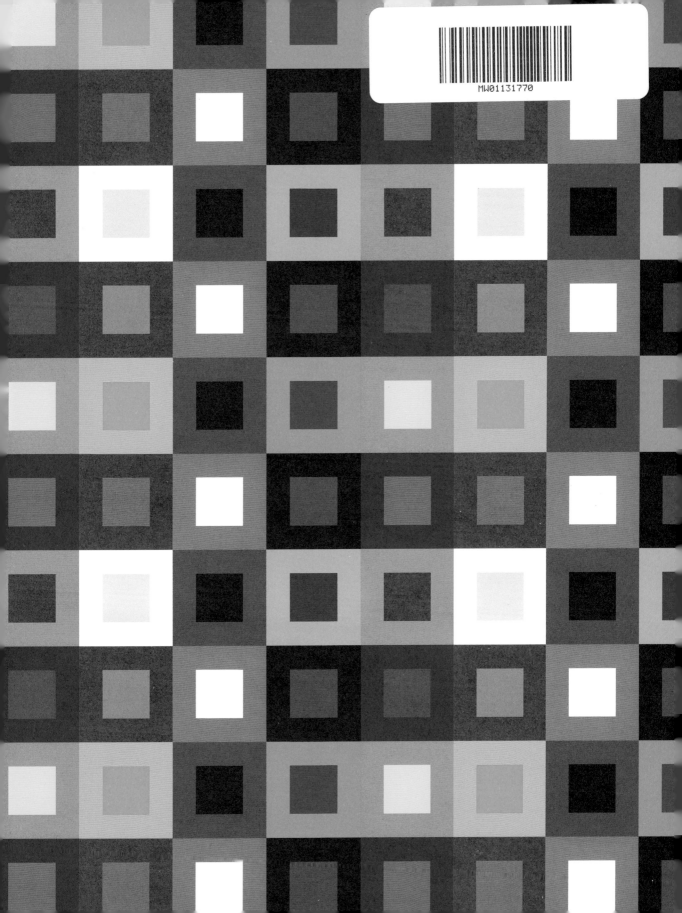

TROPE

LGBTQ+
ICONS

*A Celebration of Historical LGBTQ+
Icons in the Arts*

Illustrated by

DAVID LEE CSICSKO

Written by

OWEN KEEHNEN

CONTENTS PAGE

TELLY LEUNG

Actor & singer whose credits include Broadway's
Aladdin, Allegiance, In Transit, Godspell, Rent, *and*
Pacific Overtures, *and playing Wes on the TV show* ***Glee***

I am a performing artist and storyteller, and I've been working on Broadway (and on stages around the world) for over 20 years. But I am more than just a performer. I am a son, a friend, a spouse, a citizen of the world, a Chinese American son of immigrants, a New Yorker, a member of the LGBTQ+ community . . . and so much more!

All of the above influence the way I see the world and the art I create, and it makes me who I am. My friend David is a fellow artist in the LGBTQ+ community and with *LGBTQ+ Icons*, he has created a collection of some of the amazing artists in our community that have contributed so much to the world. All of the artists in this collection are no longer with us, so we can look at their entire life's work and try to understand not only how they have influenced later artists like me, but also the history of art and culture and made the world better.

Some of these artists have been a big inspiration to me, like Hong Kong actor Leslie Cheung and singers George Michael and Freddie Mercury. Others I've admired from afar, like choreographer Alvin Ailey and artist Frida Kahlo. Some I consider to be icons of my art, like Leonard Bernstein and Cole Porter. I was even lucky enough to work with the legendary Stephen Sondheim on the 2004 revival of *Pacific Overtures*. There are many on this list I had never heard of, and I've had a great time getting to know them, too, and learning about the rich history of the LGBTQ+ artist community.

I hope you enjoy the unique and whimsical portraits in this book and that you get to know the stories behind these incredible artists. We all have a story that makes us who we are. What is yours?

TELLY LEUNG

NEW YORK, NEW YORK (USA)

VICTOR SALVO

Founder & Executive Director,
The Legacy Project

If you read newspapers or posts on social media or watch TV news, you might have heard about "cancel culture." That's what some people call efforts to reexamine what we think we know about history.

We all need to think about history — how it's written, what's left in, what's left out — and how all of society might benefit from knowing what *really* happened. Is it important *only* to African Americans to acknowledge that celebrating people who enslaved their family members is an insult? Is it important to recognize that not everything in the past should be celebrated, if it meant that innocent people suffered? Could knowing the truth about the past help us fight for a better future for everyone? Or is it better to deny the truth if it makes some people uncomfortable?

These questions are important when it comes to how LGBTQ people have been depicted in history. If you are thinking to yourself — *"...uh, what*

LGBTQ people are there from history? I've never read about anyone in history who was LGBTQ..." — you are not alone. Nearly all LGBTQ people have been redacted from what we are taught. "Redacted" means that parts of a story are deliberately left out — or a person is left out entirely — because the one who wrote it didn't want you to know those parts. When any mention of someone being LGBTQ is removed from history, it leaves the impression that LGBTQ people simply did not exist in the past.

If you are LGBTQ (or if you have friends or family who are), think about how it feels to be left out of the story on purpose. The removal of any reference to a person in history having been LGBTQ has been going on for centuries. But today there is a movement to put back into history the parts, including LGBTQ people, that were left out.

Why does it matter? It matters because YOU should not be denied the opportunity to learn about historically significant LGBTQ people. And there are a LOT of them. How might attitudes change if kids learn from an early age that LGBTQ people have always been around and are just as important as anyone else?

If you (or anyone you know) have ever been bullied, realize that the absence of LGBTQ people who might inspire you in your day-to-day experience is at least partly the reason why some people think it is OK to pick on LGBTQ kids. It is easy to disrespect someone if everything in your life seems to indicate that LGBTQ people never existed, or never did anything that mattered.

Which is EXACTLY why this book by acclaimed artist David Lee Csicsko and historian biographer Owen Keehnen is so cool. LGBTQ+ Icons is a fantastically illustrated exploration of LGBTQ creative contributions throughout history. You are going to enjoy learning about people like artist Frida Kahlo, composer Leonard Bernstein, playwright Lorraine Hansberry, and international superstar Josephine Baker — 50 people in all. David's colorful portraits and Owen's insightful summaries of their lives will open your eyes.

It's time to rescue LGBTQ heroes from continued redaction, and "un-cancel" LGBTQ culture.

ACKNOWLEDGEMENTS

This book is in celebration and memory of Chicago critic and arts champion Andrew Patner, visionary theater director Bryan Fonseca, artist & illustrator Seth Jaben, and graphic designer Kevin Putz. A very big thank you to David Syrek, Ralph Hamilton, Jorge Partida, John Kerr, Bill Kelleher, Tracey Shafroth, Tom Bachtell, Suzanne Fleenor, Victor Salvo, and Lori Cannon for their support on this project.

And for composer and lyricist Stephen Sondheim, who was the smart soul of Broadway. His prolific output changed the course of musical theater, making him the Mozart and Shakespeare of our time.

DAVID LEE CSICSKO

For all the LGBTQ pioneers who struggled and fought so that we can enjoy the freedoms that we do today.

OWEN KEEHNEN

LGBTQ+
ICONS

PYOTR ILYICH TCHAIKOVSKY

1840 - 1893

VOTKINSK (RUSSIA)

PYOTR ILYICH
TCHAIKOVSKY

Russian composer known for his ballets
Swan Lake, The Nutcracker, and Sleeping Beauty

The symphonies of Pyotr Ilyich Tchaikovsky are played more frequently than any other classical composer. Though he showed a gift for music as a child, he was raised in a society that offered no public music education. Instead, his parents sent him to boarding school to be trained for civil service work.

As a young man, Tchaikovsky gravitated back to music. He enrolled at the new Saint Petersburg Conservatory, where the formal Western-style training distinguished him from other Russian composers of the time.

While teaching at the Moscow Conservatory, another composer suggested that Tchaikovsky write an overture based on *Romeo and Juliet*. Drawing upon his own tragic love for one of his male students, the composition became his first recognized masterpiece. Many others followed: ballets *Swan Lake* and *The Nutcracker*, the 1812 Overture, and 10 operas. In addition, the prolific composer wrote more than 100 other pieces.

In 1884, Tsar Alexander III awarded Tchaikovsky a lifetime pension for his achievements, despite rumors about his sexuality that persisted after the failure of a brief marriage. Nine days after conducting his final creation, his Symphony no. 6 (*Pathétique*), the composer was found dead at the age of 53. Authorities ruled his cause of death as cholera. Theories persist that Tchaikovsky took his own life, though many historians have rejected that claim.

Russia still refuses to acknowledge Tchaikovsky's homosexuality despite his own writings, which reveal a constant fear of his great secret being discovered.

ETHEL SMYTH

1858 – 1944

SIDCUP, ENGLAND (UK)

ETHEL SMYTH

English composer and writer who fought for a woman's right to vote; first female composer to be awarded a damehood

Though her wealthy family believed her studies were making her "unsuitably intense," Ethel Smyth refused to give up her dream of dedicating her life to music. Eventually she was allowed to attend the prestigious conservatory in Leipzig, Germany.

She made her English debut in 1890 with *Serenade in D*. Smyth composed chamber pieces, symphonies, choral works, and several operas. In 1903, *Der Wald* became the first opera written by a woman to be performed at the Metropolitan Opera.

In 1910, Smyth met Emmeline Pankhurst, a leader in the fight for women's right to vote in the United Kingdom. Smitten, Smyth pledged to give up music for two years in devotion to the cause. But first, she composed "The March of the Women," which became the battle cry of the UK's suffragette movement. When Smyth and fellow activists were sentenced to jail in 1912 for smashing the windows of politicians against allowing women to vote, Smyth conducted a prison yard performance of "The March of the Women" from her cell window with a toothbrush.

A boisterous sportswoman, Smyth published several memoirs in which she spoke frankly, but discreetly, of her love of women. Advanced hearing loss eventually ended her music career.

In 1922 she was made a Dame Commander of the Order of the British Empire, the first female composer to receive such an honor. Dame Ethel Smyth died in 1944 at age 86.

GERTRUDE STEIN

1874 – 1946

PITTSBURGH, PENNSYLVANIA (USA)

GERTRUDE STEIN

Modernist writer and poet known for the literary salon she hosted with longtime partner Alice B. Toklas

American writer Gertrude Stein and her partner Alice B. Toklas spent much of their lives living in France, becoming major influences and supporters in the development of modern art and literature.

The weekly Paris salon gatherings of Stein and Toklas attracted a long list of talents from the avant-garde art and literary worlds: Henri Matisse, Pablo Picasso, Thornton Wilder, Ernest Hemingway, Georges Braque, André Derain, Max Jacob, Guillaume Apollinaire, Henri Rousseau, Sherwood Anderson, and Ezra Pound, among many others. "Everybody brought somebody," Stein wrote, "and they came at any time . . . it was in this way that Saturday evenings began."

An acclaimed writer herself, Stein was a modernist who challenged conventional understandings of genre, narration, and form. Toklas, a fierce advocate of Stein's work, encouraged her to write *The Autobiography of Alice B. Toklas*, which brought international recognition. Additional Stein books include *The Making of Americans*, *Tender Buttons*, and *Three Lives*.

After Gertrude Stein died of cancer in 1946, Toklas spent the remaining 20 years of her life protecting and promoting Stein's legacy. The two women share a grave and headstone in Paris.

ROMAINE
BROOKS

*Distinctive painter whose work focused
on strong portraits of women*

Born in Rome to a wealthy and dysfunctional family, heiress Beatrice Goddard married gay pianist John Brooks in 1902. Though the marriage lasted only three months, Beatrice took her husband's last name, started using her middle name as her first, and became known as Romaine Brooks.

After studying art abroad and years of experimentation, Brooks eventually adopted a subdued palette dominated by grays. She primarily painted portraits. Her first solo show included two female nudes — quite bold for a female artist in 1910. During World War I, Brooks painted *The Cross of France*, which became a symbol of her adopted nation at war and was used to raise funds for the Red Cross. She later received the Chevalier medal from the French Legion of Honor for her war efforts.

Brooks made lesbian identity more visible with her renderings of androgynous, often cross-dressing women. Her subjects usually appear powerful and self-possessed. Her most reproduced painting is a grim self-portrait in top hat and riding clothes.

Brooks was romantically involved with several women and had a 50-year relationship with writer Natalie Clifford Barney. Yet Brooks maintained she was only fully herself when alone. Increasingly reclusive, she eventually refused to see even Barney. Romaine Brooks died in France in 1970 at age 96. Her work remains on permanent display at the Smithsonian in Washington, D.C.

ROMAINE BROOKS

1874 – 1970

ROME (ITALY)

NATALIE CLIFFORD BARNEY

1876 – 1972

DAYTON, OHIO (USA)

NATALIE CLIFFORD BARNEY

*Poet, playwright, and novelist who hosted
one of Paris's most popular literary salons*

Born to extraordinary wealth, Natalie Barney rebelled against the expectations of high society from an early age. Knowing she was a lesbian at age 12, she would have none of it.

At 24, Barney settled in Paris and published lesbian love sonnets anonymously. After her father died in 1902, she vowed never to conceal her identity again, saying, "My queerness is not a vice, is not deliberate, and harms no one."

In 1909, Barney started a weekly salon in her home on Paris's Left Bank. Over the next 60 years, she would host some of the Western world's greatest talents, such as Colette, Oscar Wilde, F. Scott Fitzgerald, James Joyce, and Gertrude Stein.

Barney published her last book of poetry in 1920 and afterward focused primarily on writing her memoirs and epigrams, or short witty sayings. Her only novel, *The One Who is Legion*, is a novel within a novel about a character who dies by suicide and is brought back to life as an intersex person, with both male and female traits, who then reads the book of their life.

Barney was a true feminist, an out lesbian who lived with great passion and did not believe in loving only one person. "If I had one ambition," Barney wrote, "it was to make my life itself into a poem." Barney died at age 95 in the Paris home where she had run her salon for decades.

ALLA NAZIMOVA

1879 - 1945

YALTA (UKRAINE)

ALLA
NAZIMOVA

*Renowned stage and film actress,
director, and producer whose home was
the social center of lesbian Hollywood*

After coming to the US from Russia in 1905, flamboyant actress Alla Nazimova soon triumphed on Broadway in the plays *Hedda Gabler* and *A Doll's House*.

After years of success on the stage, she began her film career. Despite being one of the highest-paid actresses at the MGM studio, her productions were often extravagant failures. Today her most popular existing films are her modernization of *Camille* and her adaptation of Oscar Wilde's *Salome*, long rumored to have a completely gay and lesbian cast and crew.

Her career options in film were already declining when the Motion Picture Production Code was introduced in 1930. Anything outside of a very strict, traditional Catholic morality was not allowed to be shown on screen. Actors whose personal lives didn't fit this code, including gay and lesbian actors, were often rejected for roles.

For years, the Garden of Alla, Nazimova's sprawling estate on Sunset Boulevard, had been a welcome home for lesbian and bisexual women in the industry, a group Nazimova called her "sewing circle."

When her fortunes waned, Nazimova went from being the owner of the estate to renting a bungalow on the property. (The new owners changed its name to the Garden of Allah.) Although she later found some renewed success on stage and in supporting film roles, she was never the star she had once been.

RADCLYFFE HALL

*Author of the groundbreaking lesbian
novel **The Well of Loneliness***

Radclyffe Hall wrote *The Well of Loneliness*, the first widely read novel in English to address lesbianism. Banned in the UK, the book became a *cause célèbre*, pitting conservatives and the legal system against medical experts and several leading literary figures.

The novel is the story of Stephen Gordon, a woman given a man's name by parents who wanted a boy. Despite social taboos, Stephen is attracted to women. She meets Mary, and the two women begin a life together. Fearing for Mary's future, Stephen pretends to have an affair. She drives Mary into a heterosexual marriage to give her the social acceptance Stephen could never provide.

The book also met resistance in the US. Police seized copies of the book, and the publisher was charged with selling an obscene publication. But this only meant more publicity for the book and increased awareness of lesbianism. By the time the case came to trial, the novel was in its sixth reprint. *The Well of Loneliness* has been continuously in print since 1928 and has been translated into over a dozen languages.

Hall knew the price to be paid for the novel's success but decided the price of staying in the closet was greater. Condemning the idea that gay people should stay silent, Hall said, "Nothing is so spiritually degrading or so undermining of one's morale as living a lie, as keeping friends only by false pretenses."

RADCLYFFE HALL

1880 – 1943

BOURNEMOUTH, ENGLAND (UK)

ALAIN LeROY LOCKE

Educator, philosopher, and writer called
"The Father of the Harlem Renaissance"

Alain Locke completed Harvard early, graduating second in the class of 1907. He became the first African American to be named a Rhodes Scholar and received a scholarship to Oxford.

After receiving his PhD in 1917, Locke became a philosophy professor at Howard University, where he remained until his retirement. He edited *The New Negro: An Interpretation*, the signature anthology of the Harlem Renaissance, and also edited *Four Negro Poets*. These important books helped make several African American authors more widely known.

Locke believed a democratic society should value uniqueness within its culture, a theory called *cultural pluralism*. Locke encouraged Black artists to embrace their ancestral and folk traditions. In the 1930s he established Associates in Negro Folk Education, a group devoted to collecting and spreading accurate information on African American culture and history. Locke also helped fellow gay African American artists like Countee Cullen and Richard Bruce Nugent.

Locke celebrated African American culture in his own writings too, including *Negro Art: Past and Present* and *The Negro and His Music*. Locke was the first Black president of the American Association of Adult Education. In 1953 he secured a Phi Beta Kappa chapter at Howard University, a milestone in African American education.

ALAIN LeROY LOCKE

1885 – 1954

PHILADELPHIA, PENNSYLVANIA (USA)

SYLVIA BEACH

1887 – 1962

BALTIMORE, MARYLAND (USA)

SYLVIA BEACH

Prominent Paris literary figure, publisher, and founder of the bookstore Shakespeare and Company

Moving to Paris in 1916 after duty as a nurse during World War I, Sylvia Beach intended to study French literature. Instead, she discovered Adrienne Monnier's bookshop, Maison des Amis des Livres.

Charmed by the store and the woman, Beach dreamed of opening a similar store in New York, but the rents were much cheaper in Paris. So she stayed and opened Shakespeare and Company, the first English lending library and bookstore in France. Business flourished. Needing more space, Beach moved her English language bookstore across the street from Monnier's French one. The women fell in love and remained together for 36 years.

In 1922, Beach and her bookshop became famous when she published James Joyce's *Ulysses*, now considered one of the most important works in English literature. Though censors in other countries had banned the book, Beach managed to get the book published by using a French typesetter who could not read English.

Shakespeare and Company closed during the Nazi occupation of France. While she was kept prisoner for six months by German troops, Beach hid her books in the vacant apartment upstairs from the shop. In 1956 she wrote a memoir of the store and Paris literary life with her personal stories about famous writers like Ernest Hemingway, Samuel Beckett, T.S. Eliot, Gertrude Stein, and Ezra Pound.

Beach died in her beloved Paris in 1962 at the age of 75.

JAMES WHALE

*Hollywood director of enduring film classics **Frankenstein** and **The Invisible Man***

James Whale spent more than a year of World War I as a prisoner of war in a German camp. Prisoners put on plays as a way to pass the time, and Whale began acting and directing. After the war ended, he continued to work in theater as an actor, set designer, and director. In 1928, Whale brought the battlefield drama *Journey's End* to the London stage with great success. The following year, he directed the play on Broadway, then moved to Hollywood to direct the film version.

Whale reached the pinnacle of his career at Universal Studios during the 1930s. He directed the horror classics *Frankenstein*, *The Old Dark House*, *The Invisible Man*, and *The Bride of Frankenstein*. In 1936, Whale made what many consider the best film version of the musical *Show Boat*. He made sure the film's African American characters were presented with realism and warmth, a rarity in films at the time.

Not long after arriving in Hollywood, Whale began a two-decade-long relationship with assistant story editor David Lewis. They were among the few gay couples in Hollywood who attended industry affairs together. Some believe Whale's openness about his sexuality harmed his career, which eventually ended in the early 1940s.

Whale spent his remaining years painting, directing plays, and living off his investments. Struggling with depression and health problems after a stroke, Whale died by suicide in 1957.

Whale understood what it was to be seen as an outsider by society. He brought that sensibility to his films, which has helped make them into enduring cinema classics.

JAMES WHALE

1889 – 1957

DUDLEY, ENGLAND (UK)

COLE PORTER

*Composer, lyricist, and writer of numerous standards as well as the music for such shows as **Kiss Me Kate** and **Anything Goes***

Cole Porter remains one of America's greatest composers and songwriters. His hit shows include the musical comedies *The Gay Divorce*, *Anything Goes*, *Panama Hattie*, *Kiss Me, Kate*, and *Can-Can*. These shows featured songs like "Night and Day," "I Get a Kick out of You," "I've Got You Under My Skin," and "Begin the Beguine."

In 1919, Porter married his close pal, socialite Linda Lee Thomas. They lived a happy, publicly acceptable life, but there was gossip about Porter being a fixture at some of underground Hollywood's most popular gay gatherings. Despite the talk, the couple never divorced, remaining close friends their entire lives.

In 1937, Porter's legs were crushed in a riding accident. Hospitalized for months, he continued to write with some success. But in the 1950s he suffered a string of tragedies that included the deaths of both his beloved mother and his wife, and the amputation of his right leg. Spirit broken and body in pain, Porter grew reliant upon alcohol and painkillers. Sadly, he never wrote another song.

He spent his remaining years in seclusion with his longtime companion, Ray Kelly. One of the most successful composers and lyricists the US has ever produced, Porter died of kidney failure at age 73. Kelly's children still receive royalties on Porter's enduring work.

COLE PORTER

1891–1964

PERU, INDIANA (USA)

ADA "BRICKTOP" SMITH

Dancer, jazz singer, and proprietor of the nightclub Chez Bricktop

Nicknamed "Bricktop" because of her red hair and freckles, Ada Smith grew up in Chicago. Performing since age five, she was a chorus girl by 14. At 16, she was on the vaudeville circuit.

She arrived in Paris in 1924, soon becoming the toast of café society. At parties she taught guests dances like the Charleston and the Black Bottom. In 1926, she opened Chez Bricktop, a queer-friendly club where all were welcome. The club showcased legends such as Duke Ellington, Sophie Tucker, and Josephine Baker (with whom Bricktop had a romantic relationship), as well as less established acts.

Smith was also a muse who inspired many famous artists and writers: Cole Porter penned "Miss Otis Regrets" for her. Evelyn Waugh, F. Scott Fitzgerald, and Ernest Hemingway all wrote about her. John Steinbeck was a fan, and T.S. Eliot wrote the poem "Bricktop" in her honor.

Fleeing Paris during World War II, she eventually opened clubs in Mexico City, Rome, and again, years later, in Paris, but none approached the success of the original Chez Bricktop.

Tired of staying up all night, Smith announced her retirement in 1961 but continued performing until shortly before her death at age 89.

ADA "BRICKTOP" SMITH

1894 – 1984

ALDERSON, WEST VIRGINIA (USA)

DOROTHY ARZNER

1897 – 1979

SAN FRANCISCO, CALIFORNIA (USA)

DOROTHY
ARZNER

*The only woman film director
of Hollywood's golden age*

After serving as an ambulance driver in World War I, Dorothy Arzner got a job at a movie studio. She started as a stenographer, a type of secretary, but over the next three years she worked her way up to script clerk and then to film editor.

The originality and power of her editing prompted the Paramount studio to hire her as a director. Arzner even helmed the studio's first "talkie" in 1929, *The Wild Party* — a remake of a silent film that Arzner herself had edited. While making the film, Arzner devised the first boom by attaching a microphone to a fishing pole and dangling it over the head of the film's star, Clara Bow.

In all, Dorothy Arzner directed 17 films between 1927 and 1943. Her films boasted capable, self-reliant heroines played by some of the era's biggest movie stars, such as Claudette Colbert, Rosalind Russell, Joan Crawford, and Katharine Hepburn. She was by all accounts the most successful woman director in Hollywood.

She was discreet about her private life, but her tailored suits, ties, and unconventionally short hair showed that she cared little about dispelling rumors. It has been speculated that her obvious lesbian identity gained her acceptance as "one of the boys."

Although romantically linked with Crawford, Ona Munson, and Alla Nazimova, the singular object of her affection was choreographer Marion Morgan, with whom she shared a 40-year relationship.

FEDERICO GARCÍA LORCA

1898 – 1936

FUENTE VAQUEROS, GRENADA (SPAIN)

FEDERICO, GARCÍA LORCA

Regarded as the 20th century's most important Spanish poet and playwright

Though he studied law, Federico García Lorca moved to Madrid from his home province of Granada in 1919 to focus on writing. He became part of an influential group of avant-garde poets and artists known as "the Generation of '27." Lorca was enamored with artist Salvador Dalí, another member of the group, although Dalí apparently rejected his advances.

Lorca's poems and plays were successful both with critics and with the public. *Gypsy Ballads*, *Blood Wedding*, *Yerma*, and *The House of Bernarda Alba* are some of his best-known works. He wrote frequently about sexual identity, even as it became more dangerous in Spain to do so. Toward the end of his life, Lorca wrote some of his strongest love poems, inspired by his romances with several men. He shared his *Sonnets of Dark Love* only with close friends, and for many years the poems were considered lost. They were finally published in 1983.

When civil war erupted in Spain in 1936, Lorca returned to Grenada to escape. Within a few months, though, Lorca was arrested and killed by the Nationalist militia. Controversy surrounds the motive for his execution. Some historians believe it was purely a political purge, though others suggest Lorca was targeted due to his sexual orientation.

In the years following his death, Federico García Lorca has come to be lionized as "the finest poet of Imperial Spain." In spite of numerous searches, his remains have never been found.

MABEL HAMPTON

1902 – 1989

WINSTON-SALEM, NORTH CAROLINA (USA)

MABEL HAMPTON

*Dancer and entertainer of the Harlem
Renaissance who became an activist and
advocate for preserving lesbian stories*

Mabel Hampton lived and worked in Harlem in the 1920s, just as the Harlem Renaissance was flourishing as the center of Black thought, culture, and literature. As a dancer and entertainer, Hampton performed at hot spots around Harlem and socialized with many LGBT entertainers who were also "in the life."

In 1920, Hampton was arrested on false charges and sent to a women's reformatory. At the time, just being a woman at a bar alone was suspicious activity, and Hampton suspected she was really arrested for being a lesbian. Hampton eventually left the stage and instead worked as a house cleaner and a hospital attendant.

In 1932 she met Lillian Foster, and their relationship lasted until Foster's death in 1978. For years Hampton was the central figure of a vibrant lesbian community in the Bronx. In 1974, she began working with the Lesbian Herstory Archives to record her story, and donated her extensive collection of memorabilia, letters, and books. She also appeared in the documentaries *Our Time* and *Before Stonewall*.

In 1984, Hampton addressed the New York Pride Rally with the words: "I, Mabel Hampton, have been a lesbian all my life, for 82 years, and I am proud of myself and my people. I would like all my people to be free in this country and all over the world, my gay people and my black people." Mabel Hampton died at age 87.

MARY
RENAULT

*Novelist best known for her books set in
ancient Greece including **The Persian Boy**
and **The Last of the Wine***

Mary Renault's father felt that education was "wasted" on women, and her mother considered female students "unfeminine." Nonetheless, this bookish girl went on to earn two degrees at Oxford, first in English and then in nursing.

In 1933, she met fellow nursing student Julie Mullard, her life partner of 48 years. Renault's first novel, *Purposes of Love*, was published in 1939. Though the plot was partly a love story between a man and a woman, Renault also explored the possibilities of same-sex love through an openly lesbian character.

Her novel *The Charioteer* dealt with love between men with a soldier's attraction to a former classmate. The book's positive and sympathetic treatment of homosexual love was so shocking at the time that years passed before a publisher dared to release it in the US.

Renault is best known for her historical novels set in ancient Greece, including *The Last of the Wine*, *The Mask of Apollo*, and *The Persian Boy*, a story told through the eyes of a beloved court eunuch. Her novels were critically acclaimed for their research and historical detail. However, for gay readers of the era, her books were among the few to present love between people of the same gender not as a problem, but simply a part of life.

Before her death at age 78, Renault told her biographer she wanted to be remembered "as someone who got it right."

MARY RENAULT

1905 – 1983

LONDON, ENGLAND (UK)

JOSEPHINE BAKER

*Dancer, entertainer, actress, civil rights activist,
and secret agent of the French Resistance*

Bisexual entertainer Josephine Baker grew up cleaning houses and babysitting for white families. After dropping out of school, she lived on the streets where her dancing led to a career in vaudeville. By 1925, Baker was the toast of Paris due to her exotic performance in the cabaret show *La Revue Nègre*. In 1927, she starred in the silent movie *Siren of the Tropics*, becoming one of the first Black women to star in a major motion picture. More films like *Zouzou* and *Princess Tam-Tam* followed.

During the Nazi occupation, Baker joined the French Underground, smuggling coded messages in her sheet music to the resistance. She later received a number of honors and medals from the French government for her bravery.

After the war, Baker returned to the US for a national tour, only to be refused service at the Stork Club in New York for being Black. In response, she refused to entertain in any segregated club or theater. Thrust into the role of civil rights leader, Baker was the only woman asked to speak at the 1963 March on Washington.

A strong believer in the gifts of a multiracial society, Baker adopted 12 children from racially diverse backgrounds. Baker died at age 68, but not before she received rave reviews in 1975 for a retrospective on her 50-year career.

JOSEPHINE BAKER

1906 – 1975

ST. LOUIS, MISSOURI (USA)

FRIDA KAHLO

1907 - 1954

MEXICO CITY (MEXICO)

FRIDA KAHLO

*Painter whose work included many
self-portraits, now widely recognized as
part of the Modern Mexican Art movement*

Frida Kahlo suffered from poor health most of her life. Born with a condition called spina bifida that affected her spine and legs, she contracted polio at age six. When she was 18, she was involved in a terrible bus accident. Kahlo was confined to a full body cast for months, and began painting to pass the time.

In 1929, Kahlo entered a tempestuous marriage to Diego Rivera, already a famous painter. For much of her career, Kahlo remained in his shadow. While married, both of them had a number of affairs; Kahlo had relationships with both men and women, including painter Georgia O'Keeffe.

By 1953, her declining health resulted in the amputation of her right leg. While in the hospital she developed pneumonia, dying just after her 47th birthday.

Kahlo's importance in the Modern Mexican Art movement was not widely recognized until years after her death. Today, her ancestral home is a popular museum and in 2001, she became the first Latina honored with a US postage stamp.

Nearly one-third of Kahlo's paintings are self-portraits. As Kahlo once said, "I paint myself because I am so often alone and because I am the subject I know best."

GLADYS BENTLEY

1907 – 1960

PHILADELPHIA, PENNSYLVANIA (USA)

GLADYS
BENTLEY

*Cross-dressing blues singer and a star entertainer
during the Harlem Renaissance*

During the Harlem Renaissance, lesbian singer and piano player Gladys Bentley was a sensation. In her trademark white tux and top hat, Bentley teased with her reputation as a "bulldagger" (butch lesbian), openly flirting with the women in the audience at venues like the Cotton Club and the Clam House.

In her act, Bentley took popular songs of the time, such as "Sweet Georgia Brown" or "Alice Blue Gown," and added suggestive lyrics. Sadly, the recordings that still exist of Bentley's performances do not include her own humorous lyrics or lesbian references. At the peak of her popularity Bentley even "married" a woman in New Jersey, though it was not legal. Her act drew audiences of all races, both gay and straight, along with many celebrities of the time.

The Great Depression severely impacted Harlem nightlife. In 1937, Bentley moved to Los Angeles where she eked out a living working in mostly gay clubs over the next decade.

The repressive climate of the 1950s made it an especially tough time to be an out, butch lesbian of color in the US. In 1952, desperate to salvage her career, Bentley published an essay in *Ebony* magazine. She claimed she had been "cured" of her lesbianism and had married a man, though whether the treatment or the marriage were real was never verified. It was a sad ending to a life otherwise lived without compromise.

ESTHER
ENG

Chinese American film director;
first female director to make Chinese films in the US

Openly lesbian filmmaker Esther Eng was born in San Francisco. She grew up a fan of the Cantonese opera and Chinese-language theaters the city had to offer. At 19, she formed a film production company with her father and altered her surname from Ng to Eng.

In 1936, she visited Hong Kong for the premiere of a movie she produced. She stayed to make the feminist film *National Heroine*, about a female Chinese fighter pilot in the war against Japan. The film was such a success that she prolonged her stay for two more years and made four more films, including *Women's World*, which showcased women in various professions.

Despite the era, Eng's lesbianism was rarely an issue. She dressed in men's attire, was open about her relationships, and received favorable press in the Hong Kong media. One news reporter even called Eng "living proof of the possibility of same-sex love."

Returning to San Francisco in 1939, she began to distribute her films to Central and South America. Two years later she became the first female to direct a Chinese-language film in the US. Eng's films tended to be romantic dramas, but with a feminist point of view.

By the 1950s, she had stopped making films and became a New York restaurateur, eventually owning five eateries in Manhattan before dying of cancer at age 55. She is remembered as a trailblazer who broke boundaries of gender, language, and race both in her work and in her life.

ESTHER ENG

1914–1970

SAN FRANCISCO, CALIFORNIA (USA)

BILLY TIPTON

1914 – 1989

OKLAHOMA CITY, OKLAHOMA (USA)

BILLY TIPTON

*Jazz musician and bandleader who presented
as male his entire adult life*

Billy Tipton grew up in Kansas City. As a high school student, Tipton studied piano and saxophone, but he had been assigned female at birth and his school forbid girls to play in the band.

In 1933, Tipton began dressing as a man to get work with jazz musicians. There were no career opportunities for women in the industry. At first, Tipton only presented as male to perform, but by 1940 he had fully assumed a male identity. Tipton hid his external sexual characteristics by coming up with a story about a serious car accident that badly injured his genitals and broke some ribs. To protect his damaged chest, he had to bind it, which kept its appearance flat.

Tipton gradually gained recognition and enjoyed some success in the 1950s and 1960s, including a recording contract.

In the early 1960s, Tipton settled down with fellow nightclub performer Kitty Kelly and they adopted three sons. By the 1970s, worsening arthritis forced him to retire.

In 1989, Tipton, who had long refused to see a doctor, had a peptic ulcer that caused a medical emergency. While paramedics worked unsuccessfully to save the 74-year-old, his son William learned his father was assigned female at birth.

After Tipton's passing, his family publicly disclosed what his ex-wife Kitty called "the best-guarded secret since Houdini."

BILLY
STRAYHORN

*Jazz composer, pianist, and arranger
who collaborated with Duke Ellington*

Billy Strayhorn was a gifted arranger, composer, and pianist. While still a teenager, he wrote both the music and lyrics for the jazz standard "Lush Life," one of the most musically sophisticated numbers of the era.

In 1938 Billy Strayhorn met Duke Ellington, and the two men collaborated for the next 28 years. Strayhorn's arrangements had a tremendous impact on Ellington's band, bringing a linear, classically schooled sound to the music. Though Ellington received much of the credit, it was Strayhorn who composed and arranged several of the band's biggest tunes, including "Take the 'A' Train."

Although his songs were among the most renowned of the Big Band Era, Billy Strayhorn's interests extended beyond the music world. He participated in the civil rights movement and was a confidant of Dr. Martin Luther King, Jr.

Billy Strayhorn lived openly as a gay man during an extremely homophobic period, an important factor in why he was overlooked for many years as an influential composer, arranger, and musician.

Strayhorn died of cancer at age 51, with his partner, Bill Grove, at his side.

BILLY STRAYHORN

1915 – 1967

DAYTON, OHIO (USA)

LEONARD BERNSTEIN

1918 – 1990

LAWRENCE, MASSACHUSETTS (USA)

LEONARD
BERNSTEIN

*Acclaimed conductor, composer,
educator, and pianist*

As a conductor, Leonard Bernstein is best known as music director of the New York Philharmonic — the first leader of a major American orchestra to actually be born in the US. He hosted *Young People's Concerts*, a televised version of the family concerts the Philharmonic had been giving for many years, and turned it into the most successful classical music appreciation program ever presented on television.

As a composer, Bernstein produced works from symphonies to ballets to Broadway shows, including the musicals *Candide*, *On the Town*, and *West Side Story*, on which he collaborated with Arthur Laurents, Jerome Robbins, and Stephen Sondheim.

Though Bernstein preferred relationships with men in his younger years, the repressive atmosphere of the era steered the career-minded Bernstein towards traditional marriage. He married actress Felicia Cohn Montealegre in 1951 and fathered three children.

The gay liberation movement may have encouraged Bernstein to become more comfortable with his desires, but his marriage and home life anchored him. Though he and his wife separated briefly in the 1970s, they remained close and did not divorce. Following her death in 1978, Bernstein began to live more openly.

In recognition of a lifetime of achievements, he received the Kennedy Center Honors in 1980. Ten years later, Leonard Bernstein died of heart failure just five days after announcing his retirement.

CHAVELA VARGAS

1919 – 2012

SAN JOAQUÍN DE FLORES (COSTA RICA)

CHAVELA VARGAS

*Legendary singer of
Mexican ranchera music*

Chavela Vargas grew up in Costa Rica but immigrated to Mexico as a teen to pursue a career in music. Vargas began performing on the streets of Mexico City. Shunning traditional gender roles, Vargas dressed as a man, smoked cigars, and drank tequila. As a singer her specialty was *rancheras*, traditional Mexican love songs for men to sing to women. With her raw vocals and acoustic guitar accompaniment, Vargas made the songs her own.

During this period, she had a brief but intense affair with painter Frida Kahlo — one of Vargas' many love affairs with women. Though a popular performer in Mexico City and Acapulco through the 1940s and 1950s, it wasn't until 1961 that Vargas released the first of her 80 albums.

When clubs stopped hiring her in the 1970s due to her struggles with alcoholism, Vargas retired and did not perform again for more than 15 years. In the late 1980s, Vargas met lawyer Alicia Pérez Duarte and managed to stop drinking, though the couple eventually parted.

In 1991, Vargas returned to the stage, performing at a club opening to great success. At age 72, it was her first sober performance. She became a muse to filmmaker Pedro Almodóvar, who described her music as "the rough voice of tenderness." She even played Carnegie Hall.

The award-winning singer formally came out as a lesbian at age 81 in her autobiography. She continued to perform until her death at age 93. Her final words were, "I leave with Mexico in my heart."

STORMÉ DeLARVERIE

1920 – 2014

NEW ORLEANS, LOUISIANA (USA)

STORMÉ DeLARVERIE

Activist, cross-dressing singer, and participant in the 1969 Stonewall Riots

Stormé DeLarverie was a mixed-race butch lesbian who traveled the country as a man despite the danger in doing so. During the 1950s and 1960s, she emceed the *Jewel Box Review*, one of the first racially integrated drag shows in North America. DeLarverie also performed in the show as a baritone-voiced drag king.

DeLarverie lived in New York's Chelsea Hotel for decades. She worked security at Henrietta Hudson and the Cubby Hole, two of the city's lesbian bars. DeLarverie considered the bar patrons her "babies" and patrolled the streets as their defender, carrying a straight razor in her sock in case they were attacked.

Various actions have been attributed to DeLarverie at the 1969 Stonewall Riots, an uprising in which LGBT people fought back after years of police raids and harassment. One story says that DeLarverie threw the first punch, though other accounts disagree. DeLarverie preferred to call the events at Stonewall a "rebellion," feeling that "riot" made it sound criminal.

Suffering from dementia, Stormé DeLarverie died at age 93 in a Brooklyn nursing home. Hundreds of her friends and admirers attended her West Village funeral.

In June 2019, DeLarverie was one of the first 50 "pioneers, trailblazers and heroes" added to the National LGBTQ Wall of Honor. Located across the street from the Stonewall Inn, the wall is part of the first US National Monument to honor LGBT history.

JAMES BALDWIN

1924 – 1987

NEW YORK, NEW YORK (USA)

JAMES
BALDWIN

Acclaimed writer, activist, and intellectual whose books include **Go Tell It on the Mountain** *and* **The Fire Next Time**

James Baldwin was a key literary voice during the civil rights era. His first novel, *Go Tell It on the Mountain*, framed an account of growing up in Harlem using many of Baldwin's own experiences. It contained ideas that became characteristic of his writing: a concern for the rights of the oppressed, and a compassionate search for human dignity amid the frustration and rage of Blacks fighting for justice.

Disillusioned by the racial prejudice in the US, Baldwin moved to France in his early 20s and lived there for most of his later life. As an openly gay man, he became increasingly vocal about discrimination against lesbian and gay people.

His novel *Giovanni's Room* was one of the first US books to deal openly with homosexuality. In his essay, "Preservation of Innocence," Baldwin addressed the charge that homosexuality was unnatural by questioning how something "old as mankind" could be anything but natural.

James wrote and lectured extensively about Black civil rights and participated in protests and marches. But he was not asked to play a visible role in the 1963 March on Washington because civil rights leaders considered his homosexuality a liability.

The man whose work exposed the ills of a nation and who helped to mold contemporary American identity died in France in 1987 at age 63.

YUKIO MISHIMA

1925 – 1970

TOKYO (JAPAN)

YUKIO
MISHIMA

*Author and playwright whose works
include Confessions of a Mask and
The Temple of the Golden Pavilion*

Yukio Mishima began writing poems and stories at an early age. He had published widely before the success of his novel, *Confessions of a Mask*, made him one of the most famous writers in Japan.

Largely autobiographical (though he later denied it), *Confessions of a Mask* was the first modern Japanese novel to deal openly with male homosexuality. Though he married and fathered two children, Mishima was attracted to men and was thought by many of his fans to be bisexual.

Around the age of 30, Mishima became preoccupied with masculinity. He threw himself into a fanatical obsession with bodybuilding, martial arts, and military training. In 1970, Mishima and four other men attempted to overthrow the Japan Self-Defense Forces. In a dramatic speech, Mishima urged the troops to revolt, to return the power back to the emperor and the military that they held before World War II. When the coup attempt failed, Mishima performed *seppuku*, traditional Japanese suicide, and died at the age of 45.

Mishima published around 40 novels, including *The Sound of Waves* and *The Temple of the Golden Pavilion*, as well as dozens of plays and essays. Yet Mishima remains an enigmatic figure both inside and outside Japan.

LORRAINE HANSBERRY

Playwright, writer and the first African American woman to have a play on Broadway

The work of Lorraine Hansberry blended art with a fierce commitment to social justice. As a girl, she moved with her family into an all-white neighborhood in Chicago, where they were met with vandalism and violence. Rather than relocate, the family sued, winning the right to stay.

Moving to New York at age 20, Hansberry married songwriter Robert Nemiroff. In 1959, her play *A Raisin in the Sun* became the first play by a Black woman to be produced on Broadway. It won many awards, and its success helped spark the African American Theater movement of the 1960s.

Sometime during the 1950s, Hansberry began to identify as a lesbian. She became an early member of the New York chapter of pioneering lesbian organization the Daughters of Bilitis. Using the penname L.H.N., Hansberry wrote several essays for the group's newsletter, *The Ladder*. Hansberry linked the struggle for gay rights, civil rights, and women's rights before words like "homophobia" and "feminism" were even widely known.

Hansberry died of cancer at age 34. Despite their divorce the previous year, Nemiroff assembled posthumous collections of her unfinished work, most notably *To Be Young, Gifted and Black*, a title drawn from a speech Hansberry made to winners of a United Negro College Fund writing contest.

LORRAINE HANSBERRY

1930 – 1965

CHICAGO, ILLINOIS (USA)

STEPHEN SONDHEIM

Master lyricist and composer who reinvented American musical theater

Born with a love of music, Stephen Sondheim studied piano at a young age. At ten, he became friends with the son of Oscar Hammerstein II, the lyricist for Broadway classics like *Oklahoma!* and *The Sound of Music*. The elder Hammerstein became a kind of father figure, mentoring Sondheim and teaching him about writing for the theater.

His big break came in 1957, as lyricist for Leonard Bernstein's *West Side Story*. Next Sondheim partnered with composer Jule Styne to write the lyrics for *Gypsy*. Sondheim followed these iconic musicals by writing both lyrics and music for another huge hit, *A Funny Thing Happened on the Way to the Forum*.

Known for his witty, complex, and conversational lyrics, his variety of styles, and his eclectic source material, Sondheim was an innovator. His work changed the face and texture of American musical theater with such productions as *Follies*, *A Little Night Music*, *Sweeney Todd*, *Sunday in the Park with George*, and *Into the Woods*.

Over his storied career, Sondheim received nine Tony Awards, eight Grammy Awards, an Academy Award, a Pulitzer Prize, and the Presidential Medal of Freedom. Sondheim was also known for his mentorship, inspiring and encouraging young artists and new talent.

Sondheim did not publicly come out as gay until he was 40, did not live with a partner until his 60s, and married in 2017 at age 87.

Stephen Sondheim was working on a new musical when he died at age 91.

STEPHEN SONDHEIM

1930 – 2021

NEW YORK, NEW YORK (USA)

ALVIN AILEY

1931 – 1989

ROGERS, TEXAS (USA)

ALVIN AILEY

*Dancer, choreographer, director, and founder
of the Alvin Ailey American Dance Theater*

Alvin Ailey discovered a love for dance as a teen. He got serious about dancing while taking classes with Lester Horton, who ran one of the first racially integrated dance schools in the US. Alvin studied with several companies before gathering together a group of Black dancers and founding the Alvin Ailey American Dance Theater in 1958.

Two years later, he debuted *Revelations*, a dance piece inspired by his grim memories of segregated Texas, as well as the blues and gospel music he grew up with. His choreography combined elements of ballet, modern, jazz, African ritual, and contemporary dance. He saw each dancer's uniqueness as important to the overall choreography. Although he wanted to provide opportunities for Black dancers, Ailey also took pride in the multicultural composition of his company.

As a result of his groundbreaking work, Ailey was the recipient of numerous honors and awards, including the 1988 Kennedy Center Honors in recognition of his contribution to American culture. The Alvin Ailey American Dance Theater is still in existence today.

After his death from AIDS in 1989, the *New York Times* wrote, "You didn't need to have known Ailey personally to have been touched by his humanity, enthusiasm and exuberance and his courageous stand for multi-racial brotherhood."

AUDRE LORDE

*Poet, activist, and champion
for social justice*

Audre Lorde fought for social justice through poetry, teaching, and civil rights activism. Describing herself as a "black, lesbian, mother, warrior, poet," Lorde argued that every part of a person's identity is equally important, declaring, "I am defined as other in every group I'm part of. . . . and my poetry comes from the intersection of me and my worlds."

She criticized white feminists who portrayed all women as a single group. She taught that racism, classism, sexism, and homophobia are linked by a failure to recognize and tolerate difference. She valued differences within groups as a strength, not as a weakness.

After being diagnosed with breast cancer in 1978, Lorde chronicled her struggle in *The Cancer Journals*. Her additional books include *Zami: A New Spelling of My Name*, and *Sister Outsider: Essays and Speeches*, both of which had a huge influence on feminist thinking and are still read and taught around the world.

Believing that acts are as important as words, Lorde co-founded Kitchen Table: Women of Color Press to promote the writing of Black feminists. She helped create Sisters in Support of Sisters in South Africa to raise concerns about Black women under apartheid, as well as activist groups in Germany and St. Croix.

Lorde took the name Gamba Adisa, meaning "Warrior: She Who Makes Her Meaning Known," in an African naming ceremony shortly before her death at age 58.

AUDRE LORDE

1934 – 1992

NEW YORK, NEW YORK (USA)

JUNE
JORDAN

*Award-winning writer, teacher, and
activist known as the "Poet of the People"*

June Jordan was born in Harlem and raised in Brooklyn, the daughter of Jamaican immigrants. As a student at Barnard College, she married a white man in 1955. The heavy intolerance the interracial couple faced ignited a fierce commitment to social justice in Jordan that defined her writing. After Jordan and her husband divorced a decade later, she also wrote frequently about her bisexuality and questioned why limits would ever need to be put on love.

Jordan began teaching in 1967 at the City College of New York. She taught at several more universities before becoming an English professor at the State University of New York at Stony Brook, where she directed the school's Poetry Center. Jordan fought for the inclusion of Black Studies in academic curricula and was a key member of the Black Arts Movement of the 1960s and '70s.

Jordan was the author or editor of over two dozen books. In addition to many books of poetry, she wrote novels, essays, and several children's titles. Jordan authored several plays and musicals and wrote librettos for two operas. She was a journalist, with a regular column in *The Progressive* magazine and stories appearing in publications around the world. She even collaborated with famous architect R. Buckminster Fuller on a redesign plan of Harlem.

As a professor of African American Studies at the University of California, Berkeley, Jordan founded Poetry for the People, a program training undergrads to take poetry to schools and community groups as a form of political empowerment.

Jordan died at age 65 after a long struggle with breast cancer.

JUNE JORDAN

1936 – 2002

NEW YORK, NEW YORK (USA)

RUDOLF NUREYEV

Superstar ballet dancer, choreographer, and actor who worked to resurrect the importance of male roles in dance

From the time his mother smuggled him into a performance of the ballet *Song of the Cranes* at six years old, Rudolf Nureyev was in love with dance. After studying in Leningrad (now Saint Petersburg), he joined the Kirov Ballet as a soloist in 1958 and quickly became one of the Soviet Union's most famous dancers.

During the company's 1961 trip to Paris, he asked the French government to let him stay and became the first dancer to defect from the Soviet Union. This made him an instant celebrity.

The same year, Nureyev danced at the Royal Ballet in London at the invitation of Margot Fonteyn, the prima ballerina there. He was quickly offered a contract and became Fonteyn's principal dancing partner — one of the greatest partnerships in the history of ballet.

Nureyev was a sensation, his technique both romantic and muscular. His dance repertoire was enormous, performing over 90 different roles with more than 30 major dance companies. He choreographed new versions of the classic ballets *Romeo and Juliet* and *The Nutcracker*, changing and expanding the roles of male dancers.

Several films were made of his brilliant performances, including *I Am a Dancer* and *Don Quixote*. He acted in several films, toured with a stage revival of *The King and I*, and was the artistic director of the Paris Opera Ballet.

Rudolf Nureyev, considered by many the greatest male dancer of the 1960s and '70s, died of AIDS at the age of 54.

RUDOLF NUREYEV

1938 – 1993

IRKUTSK (RUSSIA)

DUSTY SPRINGFIELD

1939 – 1999

LONDON, ENGLAND (UK)

DUSTY
SPRINGFIELD

*Bluesy 1960s vocalist considered one
of the best female pop singers of all time*

Dusty Springfield was born Mary O'Brien in London to a music-loving family. With her distinctive husky voice, she found early success in the folk group The Springfields, which she formed with her brother.

While touring the US, she discovered the soulful Motown sound. Inspired, she left the Springfields and transformed herself with a "far out" wardrobe, towering blonde beehive, and heavy mascara.

In 1964, Springfield released her first solo hit, "I Only Want to Be with You." The same year, she was forced to leave South Africa during a tour when she refused to sing before a segregated audience. In 1965, Springfield used a hosting gig on the TV variety show *Ready, Steady, Go!* to introduce the Motown sound to much of Britain.

In the 1960s, Springfield was known as the "White Queen of Soul" with a string of hits that included "You Don't Have to Say You Love Me," "The Look of Love," and "Son of a Preacher Man."

In 1971, Springfield came out publicly as bisexual, though she was never reported to be in a relationship with a man. In 1986, her collaboration with the Pet Shop Boys resulted in the hit "What Have I Done to Deserve This?" and introduced her remarkable voice to a whole new generation.

While recording her final album, she was diagnosed with breast cancer. After a four-year battle with the disease, Dusty Springfield died just shy of her 60th birthday. Her legacy as an extraordinary vocalist and musical talent endures to this day.

GLORIA ANZALDÚA

1942 – 2004

HARLINGEN, TEXAS (USA)

GLORIA ANZALDÚA

*Chicana poet, writer, feminist, and
co-editor of This Bridge Called My Back:
Writings by Radical Women of Color*

Gloria E. Anzaldúa moved to California in 1977 after college. She had been a schoolteacher back in Texas, but made a living in California by writing and giving lectures, sometimes teaching courses in feminism, Chicano studies, or creative writing at various universities.

Anzaldúa is best known for co-editing *This Bridge Called My Back: Writings by Radical Women of Color* with Cherri Moraga. The 1981 publication was groundbreaking not only as a collection by feminists of color, but for confronting the racism and classism in feminist thinking at the time. The book fully embraced lesbian voices and made a clear case that feminism should be inclusionary.

Her book *Borderlands/La Frontera: The New Mestiza* talked about her life growing up on the border between Texas and Mexico. The book also explored the borders between countries, languages, genders, economic classes, and within ourselves. Anzaldúa also wrote several bilingual children's books and co-edited several essay collections.

Adamant about the limiting quality of labels and all things that separate people, for Anzaldúa inclusion was essential. She was a guiding force in defining the contemporary Chicano/Chicana movement and a leader in the development of queer theory and identity.

CHARLES LUDLAM

1943 – 1987

FLORAL PARK, NEW YORK (USA)

CHARLES LUDLAM

Avant-garde playwright, actor, director, and the founder of the Ridiculous Theatrical Company

By the time Charles Ludlam received his degree in dramatic literature from Hofstra University in 1964, he was living openly as a gay man. In 1967 he formed the Ridiculous Theatrical Company.

Ludlam's satirical, experimental company soon found an audience with productions like *Conquest of the Universe* and *The Enchanted Pig*. For the next 20 years Ludlam wrote, directed, and performed (in both male and female roles) in almost all the company's productions, often with his life partner, Everett Quinton, as his co-star.

Ludlam's plays imitated everything from gothic novels to film noir, and from pulp fiction to opera. His productions were characterized by cross-dressing, double entendre, melodrama, and vicious wit. Ludlam's most popular play was *The Mystery of Irma Vep*, in which two actors play seven roles in a send-up of gothic horror novels.

He received numerous awards for his work, including six Obie Awards and a Drama Desk Award. He won grants from several large foundations and the National Endowment for the Arts.

Ludlam died of AIDS in 1987, just as his work was reaching a broader audience. In his obituary, the *New York Times* called him "one of the most prolific and flamboyant artists in the theatre of the avant-garde." In his honor, the street in front of his theater in Sheridan Square was renamed Charles Ludlam Lane. In 2009, he was inducted into the American Theater Hall of Fame.

REINALDO ARENAS

1943 – 1990

HOLGUÍN (CUBA)

REINALDO
ARENAS

*Novelist, activist, and writer whose work includes **Before Night Falls***

Born into poverty in Cuba, Reinaldo Arenas was an early supporter of the revolution that brought Fidel Castro to power in 1959. However, when the new government started to persecute homosexuals, Arenas began to condemn the revolution.

His first novel, *Singing from the Well* (1967), was his only book published in Cuba. As his writings grew increasingly critical of the government, Arenas was no longer allowed to publish in his home country. His next novel was smuggled out of Cuba to be published abroad.

In the 1970s, Arenas spent three years in prison for his writing and for being openly gay. After his release, Arenas escaped Cuba and came to the US. The 1980s were extremely productive years for him, but by the end of the decade his health had deteriorated.

Ravaged by AIDS and too sick to write, Arenas ended his own life in 1990. In a farewell letter he wrote, "My message is not a message of failure, but rather one of struggle and hope. Cuba will be free. I already am."

By the time of his death Arenas had completed nine novels, an autobiography, scores of poems, plays, and short stories, as well as dozens of political and literary essays. Among his posthumously published works were *Journey to Havana* and his most famous work, the memoir *Before Night Falls*.

KLAUS
NOMI

*Performer with extraordinary vocal range
and dramatic, otherworldly stage persona*

In his native Germany, Klaus Nomi amused his coworkers at the Deutsche Oper by singing to them from the stage following performances. In his late 20s, Nomi moved to New York City, working odd jobs and becoming part of the East Village art scene as the 1970s progressed.

In 1978 Nomi made a huge impression at "New Age Vaudeville," a one-time event over four nights at Club 57. In a skintight spacesuit with cap, Nomi sang an aria from *Samson and Delilah*, ending his performance with sound effects, strobe lights, and smoke bombs as he backed into the smoke and vanished.

Nomi was soon appearing all over the city. He gained a following for his unusual voice and music as well as his persona — bizarre theatrical performances, futuristic costumes, heavy makeup, and geometric hairdo. Nomi called himself an "alien."

David Bowie heard about Nomi and hired him as a backup singer for a *Saturday Night Live* appearance in 1979, which further accelerated Nomi's career.

Nomi released two albums in his lifetime, though additional recordings have since been compiled. Music videos for several of his songs exist, including "Nomi Song" and "Simple Man," as well as a cover of the 1960s pop hit "Lightnin' Strikes." Nomi also appeared in a handful of films. *The Nomi Song*, a documentary about his life, was released in 2004.

Klaus Nomi died of AIDS in 1983, at age 39. He was one of the first celebrities known to die from the virus. His ashes were scattered over New York City.

KLAUS NOMI

1944 – 1983

IMMENSTADT, BAVARIA (GERMANY)

DIVINE

*Campy underground superstar
of screen and stage*

Harris Glenn Milstead, who became known both professionally and personally as simply Divine, was born into a conservative Baltimore family. Bullied in high school, he was sent to a psychiatrist at 17 where he began exploring his attraction to men.

In the mid-1960s he met aspiring director John Waters, who gave him the nickname "Divine" and put him in the short film *Roman Candles*. Divine showed natural comedic talent, and his flamboyant persona evolved in several more short films before Waters cast him as one of the main characters in his first full-length movie, *Mondo Trasho*. He continued with lead roles in *Pink Flamingos*, *Female Trouble*, and *Polyester*. As Waters' outrageous movies drew wider audiences, Divine became a cult superstar.

In addition to his film work, Divine toured in the campy plays *Women Behind Bars* and *The Neon Woman* and, in 1981, launched a career as a disco diva. A huge draw in gay clubs, Divine had a series of dance hits like "Native Love (Step by Step)" and "Shoot Your Shot."

In 1988, Divine's performance in the musical *Hairspray*, Waters' most commercially successful movie, was a breakthrough that launched him into the mainstream. Just three weeks later, with another film role and a recurring sitcom role in the works, Divine died at age 42 of an enlarged heart.

In his obituary, *People* magazine declared Divine the "Drag Queen of the Century." His look inspired Ursula the Sea Witch in *The Little Mermaid*. His signature, over-the-top style has had a huge influence on the drag community that is still felt today.

DIVINE

1945 – 1988

BALTIMORE, MARYLAND (USA)

FREDDIE MERCURY

1946 – 1991

STONE TOWN (TANZANIA)

FREDDIE MERCURY

*Songwriter, dynamic performer, and lead singer
of the legendary rock & roll band Queen*

Freddie Mercury was born Farrokh Bulsara, the son of Parsi parents living in Zanzibar (now part of Tanzania), and grew up mostly in western India with relatives. He was already going by "Freddie" when the family fled a violent revolution and settled in England.

After earning a degree in graphic design, Freddie joined a series of bands, one of which became Queen at about the same time he traded his family name for the surname Mercury. With his powerful and distinctive voice, vocal range, strutting showmanship, and his talent for connecting with an audience, Mercury became a legendary rock performer.

Courageous and experimental, Queen's music covered a range of styles with songs like "Bohemian Rhapsody," "We Are the Champions," and "Another One Bites the Dust." Dozens of widely varied musical acts continue to name Queen as an influence, from rock bands like the Foo Fighters to pop acts Adele and Lady Gaga, who took her stage name from the Queen song "Radio Ga Ga."

Guarded about his private life, Mercury never came out publicly during his lifetime. He revealed he had AIDS only the day before he died, after spending his last months in seclusion. Freddie wished to be remembered for his music alone.

SYLVESTER

1947 – 1988

LOS ANGELES, CALIFORNIA (USA)

SYLVESTER

*Androgynous singer and songwriter
of the disco era*

A born performer, Sylvester James was popular as a child for performing "Never Grow Old" while standing on a milk crate at church. After his mother remarried, Sylvester fled from home, working odd jobs and running with a group of drag queens.

Moving to San Francisco in 1969, Sylvester joined the outrageous queer performance group the Cockettes. Pure electricity on stage, Sylvester continued to perform in and around the Bay Area, releasing his first album in 1973.

Five years later, after two more albums and only moderate success, Sylvester released *Step II*, which included the huge dance singles "You Make Me Feel (Mighty Real)" and "Dance (Disco Heat)." The album launched Sylvester into the disco stratosphere. The falsetto-voiced, gender-bending singer, often backed by the Weather Girls, followed those disco anthems with dance hits like "Do Ya Wanna Funk," "All I Need," and "Mutual Attraction."

Refusing to tone down his flamboyance, Sylvester was unapologetically queer, but his courage was put to an even greater test following his AIDS diagnosis. Sylvester stopped performing after learning of his illness but remained in the spotlight to bring more awareness to the disease. Nicknamed the "Queen of Disco," Sylvester succumbed to his illness at age 41.

LAURA NYRO

1947 – 1997

NEW YORK, NEW YORK (USA)

LAURA NYRO

Influential singer, songwriter, and pianist

A self-taught pianist who grew up listening to Nina Simone, Billie Holiday, Debussy, and Ravel, Laura Nyro began composing her own songs by the time she was eight years old.

In 1966, when she was 19, she sold her first song, "And When I Die." From 1968 to 1970, a number of Nyro's songs were hits, both for herself and for other artists: "Wedding Bell Blues," "Stoned Soul Picnic," "Eli's Coming," and "Stoney End." Her evocative style mixed jazz and rhythm-and-blues with street pop, gospel, and Broadway.

Several of her songs addressed social issues, such as the antiwar "Save the Country," the feminist "Women of the One World," and the environmentalist "Lite a Flame." "Broken Rainbow" was the title song of an Oscar-winning documentary about the relocation of the Navajo people from their homes in Arizona.

Nyro maintained a strong lesbian following throughout her career, partly due to "Emmie," a 1968 song in which she seems to proclaim her romantic love for another woman. Nyro always rejected that interpretation, insisting the song was about a girl becoming a woman. Nyro never publicly acknowledged her own sexuality, which included relationships with both men and women, privately referring to herself as "woman identified."

In 1977, Nyro met painter Maria Desiderio. The two women were together until Nyro's death of ovarian cancer at age 49.

LESLIE FEINBERG

1949 – 2014

KANSAS CITY, MISSOURI (USA)

LESLIE FEINBERG

Transgender activist, communist, and writer whose work includes **Stone Butch Blues**

Even by their own family, Leslie Feinberg was mercilessly abused and discriminated against for being gender non-conforming.

The prejudice and bigotry of others made it impossible for Feinberg to get steady work aside from a series of low-wage jobs. In their early 20s, Feinberg became a member of the Workers World Party and later worked as an editor and columnist for the communist organization's newspaper.

Feinberg is considered the first theorist to advance a Marxist concept of transgender liberation. This means that in the fight for human rights and equality, no one cause can be considered more important than another. After moving to New York, Feinberg became dedicated to confronting oppression of any sort. They helped organize anti-racist demonstrations, toured the US in support of AIDS patients, and rallied against war and for better treatment for all workers.

In 1993, Feinberg released the award-winning novel *Stone Butch Blues*, encouraging discussion about the complexity and fluidity of gender. Decades later the book is still widely read and praised. In addition to a second novel, *Drag King Dreams*, Feinberg's written work includes nonfiction books *Transgender Warriors: Making History from Joan of Arc to Dennis Rodman* and *Trans Liberation: Beyond Pink or Blue*.

Feinberg identified as an "anti-racist white, working-class, secular Jewish, transgender, lesbian, female revolutionary communist."

Feinberg eventually moved to Syracuse, New York, with their partner of 22 years, activist and poet Minnie Bruce Pratt. Leslie Feinberg died there at age 65 after a long illness.

LESLIE CHEUNG

Pop music star and actor whose credits include **Farewell My Concubine** *and* **Happy Together**

Born in Hong Kong, music and film star Leslie Cheung first gained attention after capturing second place in a 1977 singing contest televised across Asia. His first film and several albums did not do well, but in 1982 he signed with a new record label and had his first hit single. Cheung became a bona fide star and ushered in the Cantopop music craze.

Though Cheung had already done some TV and film acting, his success in the music world led to bigger roles. Cheung's performance in the 1986 action blockbuster *A Better Tomorrow* and its sequel the following year made him a film star. He followed this with a string of hit movies.

In 1989, Cheung announced his retirement from pop music and moved to Canada. In 1993 he starred in *Farewell My Concubine,* as a Beijing opera singer who gains fame playing female roles. *Farewell My Concubine* is the only Chinese-language film to win the Golden Palm at the Cannes Film Festival, one of the film world's most prestigious awards.

In 1995 Cheung returned to music, juggling it with his film career. During promotion for the movie *Happy Together* (1997) about a gay relationship, Cheung publicly came out as bisexual.

Cheung battled depression for years. In 2003, with his career still thriving, he took his own life. His same-sex partner, who Cheung called his "most beloved," was listed as his surviving spouse in the full-page Hong Kong obituary published by Cheung's family. More than 10,000 people attended his memorial service.

LESLIE CHEUNG

1956 – 2003

KOWLOON (HONG KONG)

KEITH
HARING

*AIDS activist and pop artist whose
graffiti-style work helped to define an era*

Keith Haring moved to New York to attend art school in 1978. Energized by new influences, he developed a graffiti-inspired art style. Wanting to expand beyond the conventional art world and bring his work to the public, Haring began his "subway drawings" — recurring chalk images drawn on expired subway advertising panels. Here Haring refined his ideas, developed his iconic urban tribal style, and added a queer sensibility.

Keith had his first solo exhibition in 1981, and soon after was the first artist to have his work shown on the huge Spectracolor billboard in Times Square. Following a 1982 solo show at a gallery in Soho, his career really took off. His art was on magazine covers and printed on fabric. Always politically active, he designed anti-nuclear posters, images for an anti-apartheid campaign, and even painted a portion of the Berlin Wall. In the late 1980s, Haring's work became synonymous with AIDS activism.

Determined to keep his art imagery affordable, Haring opened the Pop Shop, featuring merchandise with his images. His art was everywhere — from t-shirts to pins to work for companies like Swatch and Absolut.

Like Andy Warhol before him, Haring's art helped define a decade, blending consumerism, pop culture, and fine art. Sadly, Keith Haring died of AIDS in 1990 at age 31, just as a new decade was beginning.

KEITH HARING

1958 – 1990

READING, PENNSYLVANIA (USA)

DANIEL SOTOMAYOR

1958 – 1992

CHICAGO, ILLINOIS (USA)

DANIEL SOTOMAYOR

Artist, AIDS activist, and nationally syndicated political cartoonist

Daniel Sotomayor originally wanted to be an actor, and graduated with a degree in graphic arts. But when he was diagnosed with HIV/AIDS in 1988, his future went in a different direction.

Sotomayor joined the Chicago chapter of ACT UP (AIDS Coalition to Unleash Power), a direct-action activist group that fought for better treatment of people with HIV/AIDS. Using his graphic arts skills, he designed T-shirts, buttons, and protest posters — giving ACT UP's fledgling Chicago chapter a visual identity while raising needed funds.

As a member of ACT UP, Sotomayor gained notoriety for his relentless confrontation of Chicago's mayor, Richard M. Daley, over the city's AIDS budget, handling of the crisis, and inadequate education, prevention, and media programs. When the city's HIV/AIDS funding was increased, Sotomayor's confrontational, in-your-face methods were believed to be a major factor.

Sotomayor was the first openly gay political cartoonist to be nationally syndicated, or have his cartoons published in newspapers across the US. He created dozens of scathing, and often humorous, cartoons to illustrate his rage — with AIDS, government inaction, the insurance industry, the health care system, pharmaceutical companies, and even with AIDS activists themselves.

Asked about his tireless efforts, Sotomayor responded. "You just have to do what you can and don't give up. Because some day there are going to be survivors."

GREER LANKTON

1958 – 1996

FLINT, MICHIGAN (USA)

GREER LANKTON

*Muse and artist known for her ingenious
folk art dolls and elaborate art installations*

Greer Lankton grew up fascinated by dolls, and as a child fashioned them out of non-traditional materials like flowers and pipe cleaners. As she got older, she took her dolls more seriously as an art form and went to study at the Art Institute of Chicago.

Afterwards, Greer headed to New York to pursue her art. Assigned male at birth, Lankton sought gender confirmation surgery at age 21. She became a leading figure in the East Village art renaissance of the 1980s. She was a muse to photographers such as Peter Hujar and Nan Goldin.

Lankton blurred the line between folk art and fine art with her dolls, ingeniously crafted from soda bottles, umbrella hinges, and even pantyhose. Gender and sexuality were recurring themes, and her extravagant figures were often both glamorous and disturbing. Her heavily painted dolls sometimes changed from show to show, seeming to gain or lose weight, appear ill, have facelifts, or undergo sex changes.

Her final exhibit, titled *It's About Me . . . Not You*, featured pink-trimmed turquoise walls with shrines to Patti Smith, Candy Darling, Jesus, and the artist herself in a perfect reconstruction of her tiny Chicago apartment.

She died in Chicago in 1996 at age 38 but remains a unique talent in the art world. In 2017, Lankton became the first transgender artist to show at the National Gallery of Art.

LEIGH BOWERY

Performance artist, cultural influencer,
club promoter, designer, and walking art piece

Growing up a chubby and bullied outcast in the suburbs of Melbourne, Leigh Bowery spent much of his youth devouring British fashion magazines, which prompted him to move to London in 1980 to become a fashion designer. Instead, Leigh Bowery became his own greatest creation.

Combining dance, dandyism, music, and flamboyant fashions of his own design, Bowery lived as a piece of performance art. He distorted his body in different ways for an extreme appearance. Wildly creative in his style, Bowery quickly became a sensation on the queer club scene and in experimental art circles.

Smart, well-read, and interested in all forms of artistic expression, Bowery was the ideal host of Taboo, the outrageous club that was the epicenter of young and fashionable London in 1985. Bowery's groundbreaking style influenced an entire generation of artists and designers, including Vivienne Westwood, Alexander McQueen, David LaChapelle, John Galliano, and Boy George.

Drugs and HIV eventually destroyed London's underground scene. Bowery died of AIDS at age 33 on New Year's Eve 1994. Perhaps his greatest legacy was in how he lived his life. Leigh Bowery took the pain of being an outsider, owned it, exaggerated it, and ultimately reclaimed it as the ultimate badge of power.

LEIGH BOWERY

1961 – 1994

SUNSHINE, VICTORIA (AUSTRALIA)

WILLI NINJA

1961 – 2006

NEW YORK, NEW YORK (USA)

WILLI NINJA

Considered the godfather of the dance form known as voguing

Born in Queens in 1961, Willi Ninja was a self-taught dancer who loved it from an early age. In the early 1980s he became a fixture of the Harlem drag ball scene, where he was introduced to voguing and quickly perfected his own style.

Although the dance form itself wasn't new, Ninja is considered the godfather of voguing for revolutionizing it with his clean, angular moves and bringing the dance form to the mainstream. In 1989, he worked with Malcolm McLaren on the video for the dance single "Deep in Vogue." The following year, Madonna's "Vogue" topped the charts in more than 30 countries. The song's video, inspired by Ninja's signature style, helped to spread the dance worldwide.

Ninja is prominently featured in Jennie Livingston's 1990 documentary *Paris is Burning*, which chronicled the Harlem drag ball world and showcased some of the key people in ball culture. Ninja is also one of the subjects of the 2006 documentary *How Do I Look*.

Ninja was featured in two Janet Jackson music videos and the Marlon Riggs short film *Anthem*. He worked with Jean Paul Gaultier and other fashion icons. Ninja worked as a runway choreographer, training models how to move on the catwalk. He taught celebrities how to pose for the paparazzi, and even opened his own modeling agency in 2004.

Ninja founded the House of Ninja in 1982. The House was part extended social family, part dance troupe. Ninja remained the Mother of the House of Ninja until his death at age 45 from AIDS-related heart failure.

GEORGE MICHAEL

*Singer, songwriter, and producer who remains
one of the best-selling music artists of all time*

Grammy Award-winning recording artist George Michael found fame when he formed the pop duo Wham! with school friend Andrew Ridgeley. Wham! was an immediate success. In their five years together the duo put out a string of hits, including "Wake Me Up Before You Go-Go" and "Careless Whisper." In 1985, they made history as the first Western pop group to perform live in China.

Blessed with good looks, a powerful and emotive voice, and dynamic stage presence, George Michael easily transitioned to success as a solo artist. His debut solo album, *Faith*, was a huge hit, producing a string of #1 singles. His next album, *Listen Without Prejudice, Vol. 1*, got positive reviews but did not sell as well, resulting in a legal battle with his record label that kept him from putting out another album for more than five years.

Michael struggled with periods of depression and addiction, and several times sordid headlines threatened his career. In 1998, Michael publicly came out as gay after an arrest for lewd conduct. He later turned the incident into the hit dance single "Outside."

Michael performed duets with legends from Aretha Franklin to Elton John. He lent his talents to anti-famine efforts with the singles "Do They Know It's Christmas?" and "Last Christmas." He played many benefit concerts.

Michael had a generous spirit and donated hundreds of millions of pounds to various causes and charitable organizations. A number of charities and individuals revealed after his death that Michael had privately or even anonymously given them financial support.

The pop artist who sold over 100 million albums in his career died on Christmas Day 2016 at the age of 53.

GEORGE MICHAEL

1963 – 2016

LONDON, ENGLAND (UK)

LGBTQ+

ICONS

GEORGE MICHAEL

1963 – 2016

LONDON, ENGLAND (UK)

LGBTQ+

ICONS

DAVID LEE
CSICSKO

is an award-winning artist and designer whose distinctive artwork, stained glass, and mosaics beautify train stations, hospitals, and universities across the Midwest and East Coast. His many credits include designing the Obamas' White House Christmas in 2012. David's lively illustrations can also be seen in *The Skin You Live In* from the Chicago Children's Museum, now in its 16th printing. Through his use of color, bold graphics and playful patterns, David Lee Csicsko celebrates the richness and diversity of life.

OWEN
KEEHNEN

— queer author, activist, and grassroots historian — has written several fiction and nonfiction books and has been published in dozens of magazines and anthologies worldwide. He is a co-founder of The Legacy Project, a Chicago-based LGBTQ history, arts, and education organization. Owen was inducted into the Chicago LGBT Hall of Fame for his dedication to fostering LGBTQ culture and preserving its past.

LGBTQ+
Resources

Centers for Disease Control Youth Services
cdc.gov/lgbthealth/youth-resources.htm

COLAGE
colage.org

GenderCool Project
gendercool.org

GLSEN
glsen.org

interACT
interactadvocates.org

It Gets Better
itgetsbetter.org/get-help

Lambda Legal Defense Youth Issues
lambdalegal.org/issues/youth

The Legacy Project
legacyprojectchicago.org

National Runaway Safeline
1800runaway.org
1-800-RUNAWAY

National Suicide Prevention Lifeline
suicidepreventionlifeline.org
1-800-273-8255

PFLAG
pflag.org/lgbtq-people

Stomp Out Bullying
stompoutbullying.org/lgbtq-bullying

Strong Family Alliance
strongfamilyalliance.org

Teen Central
teencentral.com

Trans Lifeline
translifeline.org

The Trevor Project
thetrevorproject.org

© 2022 Illustrations by David Lee Csicsko
© 2022 Text by Owen Keehnen

LCCN: 2021953097
ISBN: 978-1-9519631-1-8

Printed and bound in China
First printing, 2022

David Lee Csicsko's illustrations from *LGBTQ+ Icons* are available for purchase. For inquiries, go to trope.com or email the gallery at info@trope.com.

+ INFORMATION:
For additional information on the Trope Edition Series, visit trope.com